PASSING ON YOUR
Legacy of Love

Scrapbooking with a Purpose

Leave the story of who you are to those you love.

MARCI WHITFORD

Passing On Your Legacy Of Love

Scrapbooking with a Purpose

"Leave the story of who you are to those you love."

by Marci Whitford

Published by Reminders Of Faith, Inc.
518 Overhead Drive
Moon Township, PA 15108
orders@remindersoffaith.com
http://www.remindersoffaith.com

President: Sandra L. Joseph
Vice President: Kathy Brundage
Art Director: Beth Beiter
Editor: Tonja M. Brossette
Graphic Designer: Beth Beiter
Illustrator: Gina Hurst
Scrapbook Page Layout Artist: Marci Whitford

Paper Broker and Advisor: Nancy Guthrie
Photography by Paul Palermo, Palermo Imaging, Warrendale, PA

LEGACY lyrics by Nicole Nordeman, Copyright: ARIOSE MUSIC.
Publisher: ARIOSE MUSIC, Copyright © 2004 Music Services. All rights reserved.

Scripture taken from the HOLY BIBLE: NEW INTERNATIONAL VERSION®.
NIV®. Copyright © 1973, 1978, 1984 by International Bible Society.
Used with permission of The Zondervan Corporation.

ISBN 0-9748160-1-9
Library of Congress Control Number: 2004092926

Dedication

This book is lovingly dedicated to the memory of my mother, Pamela. She is the inspiration behind this concept, and I take comfort in the truth that I will know her someday in Heaven! I would also like to dedicate this book to all women who want to leave a legacy of their lives for their children, and to those searching to discover details of their own mothers' lives.

Acknowledgements

Thank you, Christ my Savior, for the ideas and thoughts behind such a special album. Ty, my supportive husband, thank you for believing in me and giving me the time to pull my thoughts together and create these pages. Cameron and Coleton, thank you for being understanding on those days you had to play more on your own, and for being my reasons to create this book! Sandra, I thank God for you and all of the advice and support you have given to me for this book - I thank the Lord for bringing you into my life. Kathy, thank you for your encouragement and nudge to create this book, and for giving me deadlines! A special thanks to all of my family and close friends - your prayers and support have meant the world to me. Amy, thank you for encouraging me a few years ago to follow my dreams. Thank you, Nicole, for your encouragement when some of these projects became overwhelming, and when I needed you as a second set of eyes for my pages. A warm and special thanks to my first workshop participants in Orlando 2½ years ago when this book was merely an idea. I have not forgotten you!

And finally, thank *you* for choosing to read this book. Sharing this wonderful message with you means more than I could ever put into words.

Dear Friends,

Thank you for choosing to read this book. My hope is that you find encouragement and ideas with which to complete your special project. It may be beneficial, as you make your way through the pages of this book, to understand this work's inception.

One of the fundamental objectives throughout my life is to be real with those around me. I am confident that one day, my children will have a deep desire and need to really understand who their parents are, on a somewhat different level than they know during our day-to-day interactions with one another. As a result of my own desire to have known my mother on a deeper level, I made the decision to create a scrapbook album focusing solely on myself and proposed expressly for my children. When they are older, they will receive these albums that embrace everything they might possibly want to know about me.

After my mother lost her battle to breast cancer when I was 8 years old, I never really put a lot of deep consideration into the person she was, or thought to examine her personality or her values. As I grew and eventually evolved into a wife, then a mother of my own children, I found myself contemplating who my mother was, what she stood for, her values and beliefs. I could have asked family members for the answers I was looking for, but somehow, I knew that those answers would have fallen short of my mother's own words. Although my children may not yet be ready for many of the aspects of my life I have to share with them, I feel a powerful sense of contentment and peace knowing that they will be blessed by this album that was hand-created by me, and is filled to the brim with essential details and self-made creations motivated exclusively by my love for them - an account that portrays my life, and my legacy, intended to be passed on to them.

As I created a workshop based on this concept, I quickly discovered from my participants that, indeed, women of all ages, mothers and mothers-to-be, were taking my workshop because the outcome was just what they longed to accomplish for their own family members. They had a desire to create something that truly represented themselves, something they could pour themselves into for their children, but were unclear on how to accomplish such a task.

I have created this book to help you take each step in crafting this special album to pass along to your own children. For me, I find comfort in knowing that my legacy will be passed on to them, and that this tremendous work of love may influence them to pass on their legacies to their own children some day. I hope that you enjoy the pages I have composed for you, and that you find fulfillment in opening your hearts into creating your own project, knowing you'll be giving your children an extraordinary and unique gift they will cherish forever.

Your friend,

Marci J. Whitford

Table of Contents

Forward

In the spring, I met a woman through the Internet on a breast cancer message board who quickly evolved into a friend. Her story was one to which I immediately related, as she is a 28-year old mother of two, facing the difficult trials of a breast cancer diagnosis and all of the complex aspects that surround this devastating disease. As a 28-year old mother of two myself, I was immediately touched by the fact that her story was a parallel to my past and a testimony to the significance of my mission to reach others who have been called to this extraordinary challenge.

At the age of 32, my mother died of breast cancer, leaving behind two young children. I felt compelled to write to my new friend and share my story with her. I wanted to touch her with my experience of living the life of those who find themselves on the other side, and to impart to her that I could, on a personal level, connect with the feelings of her children through her process and the difficult emotions that are inevitable, but often overlooked. In a carefully and protectively construed way, I wanted to share with her that, while she had a tremendous chance of survival, it was crucial for her to begin the course of journaling her life, and her experiences, in a loving endeavor to ensure that her children would someday be left with not only memories of their mother, but with a tangible and detailed legacy of her life and who she was. Although I was somewhat reluctant, my heart prevailed and I opened my heart to her in the form of a letter.

A few weeks later, I received an E-mail from my friend expressing how grateful she was to have received my letter. She told me that she had begun the journey of creating a scrapbook album, journaling the facets of her life. Through this process, not only will my friend be speaking to her children through the pages in her album for years to come, she will be documenting her own journey through this difficult experience. I marvel at how positive she remains and how her children are gaining an invaluable lesson from her grace in coping with such a difficult process, as well as her generosity in ensuring that they will be left some day with a part of her – a part that they can see, read, touch and feel. By witnessing this chapter of her life, her children will be left with an insight of what she stood for. This will become, in the end, a part of her legacy.

Section One

Laying Some Ground Work
How to Get Started

To get started, there are some preliminary steps you will need to take that are essential in getting your album in progress! In this section, you will find helpful tips on what type and size of album to use for your project, how to decide the number of albums to create, and ideas for a range of styles you may want to incorporate into your album. You'll also find suggestions on shopping for supplies and various ways to organize the photographs you will be integrating into your album.

Motivate yourself! You may find yourself in need of some encouragement to get you started. Try posting a picture of your children in your work area. My niece gave me a calendar last year as a Christmas gift that contains pictures of my children, one for each month of the year. This calendar remains in my office and serves as a source of continuous inspiration each time I sit down to work on my albums. Posting photographs of your own children will likely encourage you when you become tempted to postpone your project.

Will each child get an album of their own?

You will need to decide if you are going to create a separate album for each of your children, or one album for them to share. This will help you determine the size of the album you wish to create. There are many ways to help you avoid creating the same pages more than once if you decide on multiple albums for this project. For example, you may decide to create a page about yourself entitled, "100 Things I Love." This page could be colored copied for each album to avoid duplicating your effort by hand. A page such as, "10 Things I Love About You," on the other hand, would be one you would want to personalize, as you most likely have different things you want to say to each child. Decide as you go along which pages can be color copied and which merit individual creation, ensuring that you allocate the color-copied pages equally to each child.

What size album to use? Now that you have decided how many albums you would like to create, you should decide on the size of the album. There are many sizes on the market to choose from, one of which will be perfect for your project. Below are some things to consider as you make your decision on the size of your album:

- Choose an album that allows you to move pages easily;
- Choose a size that isn't too bulky or cumbersome to store;
- A 12 x 12 album may be too large for this kind of project, while a 5 x 7 or 6 x 6 album may not provide enough space to include all of the details you wish to share. For me, an 8 ½ x 11 album proved to be just right for this type of project.

Next, you'll need to decide what type of album to use. I chose a leather, three-ring album for my project because I know I will be rearranging pages frequently as I progress.

Common elements: Your next step will be deciding on how you would like your album to flow. Since this album is theme-based, each page should show some uniformity. I chose to accomplish this by creating my album in one, consistent color. I chose pattern papers that coordinate in color and design and harmonized well together visually. As you progress through this book, you will see page examples of different color schemes and

ideas to help you decide on a theme that best represents you and your personality.

When deciding on the style of your pages, you may wish to create each page with the same border or layout. I utilized many of the same products throughout my album, such as beads and ribbon. These embellishments helped to maintain similarity in my album pages while creating a unique design for each.

many years. Think about a practical album with a nice embellishment charm, keeping in mind the purpose behind creating this album. You don't have to focus on impressing others with your scrapbooking skills, rather to make it appealing enough for you to feel a sense of creative accomplishment when it is complete. Progressive styles and techniques can yield a beautiful album, however; take care to ensure that these elements will withstand the test

...this is not about creating the most beautifully intricate scrapbook of your life, but about sharing your life stories with your children, who will cherish every page...

All of the example pages in this book have been created from paper by Reminders of Faith. You may visit them at www.remindersoffaith.com to browse through their entire line of paper, tags, and embellishments. They offer a terrific line of products that allow you to use the same designs of pattern paper, but in different colors.

Decide what style to portray: While a trendy album with a variety of chunky techniques is attractive, consider that it may not endure over the course of

of time, and bear in mind that your style should be classic rather than trendy, as your album will be viewed for many years by your children. For some scrapbooking projects, less is more!

Throughout this book, you will see pages created with simplicity, and others that appear to have entailed a little more time and effort in the design. I have crafted this book for you as a resource for simple ideas and inspiration from which to create and share your personal story with your children. Too often, I pick up scrapbook resources and magazines to find myself overwhelmed at the details, and apprehensive at my ability to create my own projects as beautiful as those I am viewing. Although these elaborate pages can be inspiring, they can also be intimidating and feel unattainable. I made the decision to take the pressure off of myself and to follow what comes naturally in telling my children my story. I hope that you find you can do the same, keeping in mind that this is not about creating the most beautifully intricate scrapbook of your life, but about sharing your life stories with your children, who will cherish every page, even in its most basic simplicity.

Shopping:

The next step will be to visit your local scrapbook store and shop for supplies! There are many resources available, including Reminders of Faith at www.remindersoffaith.com. After I chose my color scheme, I purchased 4 or 5 different designs of pattern paper that complimented each other. I then picked out a few different shades of cardstock that would flatter the paper I had chosen. I found various embellishments, fibers, and materials I felt would best represent me. If you intend for your album to be a work in progress for years, remember to purchase an extra supply of the cardstock and pattern paper you have chosen, as it may not be available many years from now.

Motivational elements:

Find what motivates you, and use it to its full advantage! Perhaps you enjoy listening to certain music that helps trigger your creative juices. Play it! Maybe your thoughts begin to bloom when you are exercising. Get moving! When I work on my album, I find myself most inspired in a quiet atmosphere (listening to my kids argue isn't the most hospitable surrounding from which to gather inspiration for this project!). Whatever you find inspires you, whether it is music, prayer, or an early morning jog, use it to evoke your emotions and motivate you to move ahead on your project!

Photo time:

Sort through all of your photographs! I have a photo box full of pictures, and I decided to go through it and choose my favorites before I started my album. I chose my most cherished photographs, including one of myself as a child, as children are often surprised to see for themselves that we were once kids, too! I compiled a stock of about 20 photographs, a process that has saved me time in inevitably rummaging through my photo box numerous times to find a picture I want to incorporate. Gathering them in advance will save you time as you find yourself absorbed in your project. Because this album is created around your journaling and thoughts, it is often less complicated to add pictures when you need them.

Take additional photos:

Now that you have a small reserve of your favorite photographs handy, you may find that you need more to fill in the gaps. Compile a list of pictures you would like to include, and take them all at once or a few at a time. For example, make sure you have a picture of yourself with each of your children. A more expanded list of these ideas can be found at the end of this book.

Section Two

You are now ready to begin!

In the following section, I will show page examples of my own album and my thoughts on creating them for my children. Feel free to incorporate your own unique ideas and creative thoughts into your album, or use the following layouts as a guideline.

An Introduction Page

Dear Coleton,
I am making this book for you because I love you so much. I want you to know many things about me as your mother and as a person. I have been so blessed to have you as my son, and there is so much I want to share with you through this book. I know that someday you will cherish this and enjoy the things that I have shared with you. This picture of us together is what we looked like when I started this book for you, at age 3 and 26.
I love you and I thank God that your life was shared with me.
Love,
Mom

To the left and the facing page are some examples of an introduction page. An introduction page is important because it conveys to your child why you are creating this album for him. In mine, I included my age at which I began this album, as well as the ages of each of my boys at the time. I created a separate introduction page for each of my sons and incorporated a photograph of myself with each of them. I will worry about pages for my future children when they arrive! If you have more than one child, you may choose to create the same page repeatedly, or make each introduction page carry a different style altogether.

Dear Cameron,

I am making this book for you because I love you so much. I want you to know many things about me as your mother and as a person. I have been so blessed to have you as my son, and there is so much I want to share with you through this book. I know that someday you will cherish this and enjoy the things that I have shared with you. This picture of us together is what we looked like when I started this book for you, at age 5 and 28. I love you and I thank God that your life was shared with me.

Love,
Mom

Leaving My Legacy

My motivation behind creating this page is a song that means a great deal to me. When I hear it, I think of what my legacy will mean to my children, and am prompted to ask myself if I am living a legacy that I would be proud to pass onto my children. As the title of the song is, "Legacy," by Nicole Nordeman, I thought it would be appropriate to utilize this page to tell my children that my legacy – what I want to pass down to them, what I want to live out each day of my life – is written on the pages of this album. It is comforting to know that my kids will not have to wonder what I was about someday. The answers are all here for them through the pages of this album. Ask yourself: "What do I want to pass down to my children?"

Dear Children,

Through this scrapbook album I leave my legacy. I pray it is a legacy I can be proud of, God is proud of me for, and you all can find strength, warmth, and helpful ways to live your lives by. Everything I have learned I have learned from my Heavenly Father.

I have included the words to a song, "Legacy", to this page because it says, better than I could, what I strive for my legacy to be.

I don't mind if you've got something
nice to say about me
And I enjoy an accolade like the rest
And you could take my picture and hang it in a gallery
Of all the Who's Who's and So-and-So's
That used to be the best at such and such
It wouldn't matter much
I won't lie, it feels alright to see your name in lights
We all need an "Atta boy" or "Atta girl"
But in the end
I'd like to hang my hat on more besides
The temporary trappings of this world
I want to leave a legacy
How will they remember me?
Did I choose to love?

Did I point to you enough?
To make a mark on things
I want to leave an offering
A child of mercy and grace
Who blessed your name unapologetically
And leave that kind of legacy
I don't have to look too far or too long awhile
To make a lengthy list of all that I enjoy
It's an accumulating trinket and treasure pile
Where moth and rust, thieves and such will soon
Enough destroy
Not well-traveled, not well-read
Not well-to-do, or well-bred
Just want to hear instead
Well done, good and faithful one
I don't mind if you've got something nice to say about me

Written by Nicole Nordeman

Dreams & Goals

Tell your children about your dreams of the past, and detail your dreams for the future! Not all of your journaling has to be profound. If you dream of having a boat someday, tell them! If your dreams encompass having a lifelong, meaningful relationship with your grandchildren someday, don't leave that out! If you've always dreamed of being a stay-at-home mother and fulfilled that dream, incorporate that into your journaling, and express how meaningful that accomplishment has been. Tell your children what you feel. Communicate with them what is inside of you.

You may choose to make this a "goals" page instead. Simply make a list of the goals you hope to accomplish during your lifetime, and check these goals off as they are accomplished. It's not as important that these goals are all achieved as much as it is that your children see that you have them.

I added a pocket to this page so that I can journal more goals and dreams throughout the years. All I have to do is write them on acid-free journal paper as I think of them, then place them in the pocket.

As a little girl I played "house" a lot. All I really wanted to do was grow up and get married, have a family, and be a teacher. When playing school, I always was the teacher!

As a young woman in college, I was studying to become a teacher of el. Ed., but I never really knew if that was what I wanted to do. I always had feelings of being at home and doing something from there, I just didn't know what.

As a mother, being a better Mom is what I continue to strive for. I always wanted to stay home with my children and still bring in at least a small income for our family. That is very important to me. Later it all fell into place when I discovered scrapbooking and preserving family memories. My dreams came true when I relied on the Lord!

Now my dreams are, as a family, to love one another and to be a very close family. I dream of our close relationships and how they will grow through the years. I dream that we will travel and laugh together through life. I dream that we all will love the Lord with all our hearts and choose His will for our lives.

I also dream of adopting my daughter from China! I can't wait to fulfill that dream! I love to sit and think about how life will be with her and all of us together!

On a not so deep note, I dream of a very hospitable home, on a lake that we can boat on. I have always loved to go boating. I want my children to like the water and learn how to ski. I dream of traveling with your daddy someday, and just enjoying each other's company. I pray that God will bless us all with long, healthy, happy lives.

To my children: never give up on your DREAMS, never stop believing!

Mom's Favorite Things

Sharing your favorite things with your children is very important, as this is a part of your legacy they will surely want to know about! For me, knowing my mother's favorite things would have allowed me to discover some of the things we may have had in common. I like fall weather, eating caramel apples, pumpkin pie, and S'mores. Would she have liked any of these things enough to call them her favorites as well?

As you can see from the example, I chose to write my favorite things in various styles around the page so that I can append to this page as needed. You may first want to begin a list on a separate piece of paper and add to it as you think of ideas before creating your page. I also chose to adhere pictures of some of my favorite things under the vellum. This was such a simple page to create, yet it encompasses so much of my personality because the words are written in my own handwriting. I also added a few charms representing some of my favorite things, such as the camera, because I love taking pictures! Whatever your favorite things are, find embellishments to represent and embody your personality!

Since our "favorite things" will likely change over time (my birthday may not be a favorite day of mine years from now!), you may choose to create another page like this in the future as you age. For example, you may decide to create a page entitled, "My Favorite Things During My Childhood," and add lists separated into categories such as, "Teens," "Twenties," "Thirties," and so forth. Although I may or may not be adding these details to their albums when I'm 70 or 80 years old, I decided to save myself some time and create the page now. Another simple step I took was to leave the vellum loose on the second page so that I could easily add more pictures at a later time.

You may also want to think about creating a page that describes to your children what annoys you. For example, loud eaters, having my feet touch the slimy bottom of a lake, the toilet paper installed on the roll the "wrong" way, and clutter are all things that annoy me. I also chose to use this page as a means to send a message to my children that we all have annoyances, but that we should not dwell on them. Rather, we should make our days positive!

Ask Yourself—

What do you like to eat or drink?

What are your favorite colors?

What is your favorite car?

What are your hobbies or activities?

What makes you angry or annoys you?

What makes you laugh or gets you excited?

Making a Difference

Since I have so many favorite things, I thought I should also show some true colors in a different direction. I feel the need to tell my children about the things that annoy me so that they know I do get upset at times, too. In my layout, I listed some things that annoy me, but I didn't highlight the list extensively. Instead, I wanted to show a more fruitful way of channeling negative energy into positive. I wanted to use my album to drive home a message to my children that ill feelings do nothing, while positive attitudes and servant hood do great things.

With this in mind, I listed some things that I have done and anticipate doing in the future to make a difference in my small world. I explained to my children that my list will likely grow as I get older. By seeing this, my hope is that they follow in my footsteps and find ways to donate of themselves throughout their own journeys.

Journal and ask yourself some questions: What do you stand for? What subjects interest you? Do you find yourself concerned with certain issues that motivate you to do something to make a difference in your household, your town, or your country? What do you hope your children learn from you?

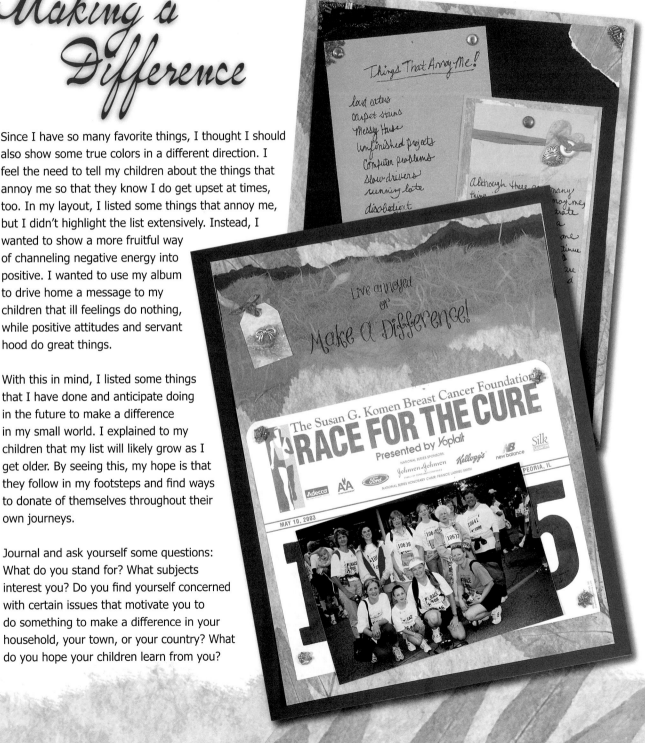

Passing On Your Legacy Of Love

Mom's Challenges Through Life

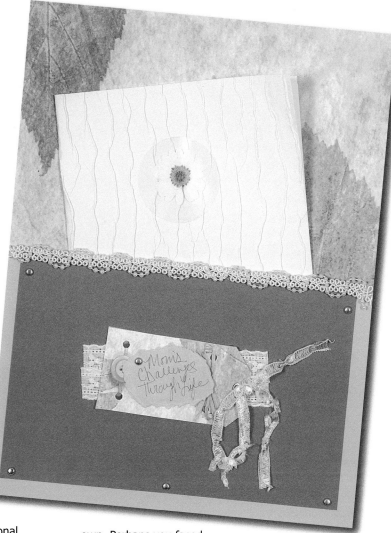

For this page, I created another pocket that would hide my journaling while allowing me to add more over time. I created a small, handmade journal that will allow me to enter thoughts as needed, and then slip them into the pocket on the page. For much of my journaling, I use acid-free paper from a journal and tear it out to place into the albums. When I journal in this way, I make sure I incorporate my own handwriting rather than utilize the computer.

It is essential that your children have access to your handwriting, no matter how substandard you feel it is! Have you ever seen a loved one's handwriting on a card and it made you feel close to them? I have a friend whose husband was recently overseas for 9 months. During this time, the need for his signature was required on various financial documents, which she sent to him through the mail. When she received them back, she discovered that seeing his signature in front of her, knowing that he had held those papers and signed them with his own hand, made her incredibly emotional since she had not seen him in months! In turn, it made her feel very close to him for that moment. I have a 90-year old great grandmother and, although her handwriting is becoming difficult to read, I love seeing it. I know that when she isn't here with me, I will cherish seeing her writing in the cards she has given to me over the years.

We all have challenges through our lives, and it is important that our children know about them. This is where they will discover your coping abilities and how you endured your challenges. Through sharing this, you will help them find the courage they need to get through their own. Perhaps you faced the challenge of working your way through college and want to share your experiences as a means to encourage them to do the same. Perhaps you were confronted with trials as a single, working mother and would like to share words about those years with your kids. One thing I will share with my children is what gave me the strength I needed to live without my mother. Although I hope they will never have to live with a loss of this magnitude, what helps me overcome my challenges is something that may help them cope with loss during their lives.

19

Mom's Childhood

Often, kids forget that we were once children, too! I highly recommend that you include a layout about your childhood, sharing where you were born, who was important in your life, and including details about your hometown. What were your fondest memories of childhood? What did you learn from those close to you? How did you feel about your siblings? Perhaps you have some challenging aspects of your life to share. Did you and your parents get along well? Don't be afraid to journal to your children about the difficult things you went through in life. This will show them that you, too, endured tough times, as they inevitably will. Avoid giving the impression that you had a perfect life, as this could result in feelings of inadequacy during the times in their own lives when things become challenging. They will likely find strength in how you faced and coped with your life challenges.

On my Childhood Page, I portrayed the town I grew up in. I included details about the houses I lived in, thoughts about my family members and what I gained from each one. I also described those who influenced

mom's childhood

I was born and raised in a medium sized town called Pekin, IL. Pekin is a town consisting of a "mixture" of people. High, medium, low incomes. Mostly blue collar, hard working people.

Pekin has great parks and landscaping. Whenever Pekin decides to do something, they go all out. The fireworks here are the best in IL, and Pekin puts on one fantastic Marigold Festival every year.

I never really minded growing up here. I have always had good friends and fun times here, but I do have to say that I have never felt "at home" in Pekin. Maybe time will make those feelings different since it is where Dad and I are choosing to make our home for now.

I really only remember growing up in two homes. One was a small ranch style that I always enjoyed. I have many great younger childhood memories there. The other home was in part of town called Sunset Hills. It was a split level home with plenty of room for us. I'll always cherish the first home because of the memories with my mother there. The second home has many great memories too, mostly having to do with friends, boyfriends, and little baby sisters.

I liked having a big brother to look up to, and when I was in Jr. High and High School I enjoyed having little sisters too. I would never change their arrival into my life. I look forward to many years watching their lives bloom.

I owe my whole life to God, Jesus Christ, my Savior. After my mother's death I just remember God carrying me through my whole entire life. I depended on Him for everything, kind of like my parent. I really would say that He shaped and impacted my life more than any person or thing. I really feel like he "raised" me.

my life in a profound way as a child and, as that bit of journaling could only cover so much, I added an extra page equipped with a pocket to hold more childhood stories. I love pockets! They allow you to add more journaling over the years as you think of more things to share with your children without having to rearrange your album to allow room for more details.

Ask Yourself

Explore your background! Sit down, close your eyes, and go back through time in your mind. Think about each person who was primarily involved in your life.

What has happened to make you who you are?

What do you believe?

When you were younger, what did you think you would accomplish when you got older?

What do you hope to accomplish in the future?

Mom's School Stories

This may be one of the pages in your scrapbook you would like your children to see before you give them the album. Perhaps you have reasons for showing them this page as they go through school so they can see what this period of time was like for you.

Do you have silly school stories you would like to share with your children? Share them on a page about school memories! Maybe you would like to include encouraging notes that helped you get through the more trying stages of school. I included one story about my biggest fear in school. To find out what it was, attend my workshop related to this book!

What do I want my children to gain from reading my childhood stories? I want them to recognize that I was not always a mother, and that, once upon my younger days, I, too, did fun and crazy things! You will notice that I used a pocket to hold these stories, which I wrote on small pieces of cardstock. This allowed me to include several pieces of journaling on one page so my children will be able to simply pull them out as they wish to read them. They can remove them completely from the page protector, or you can create a small opening in the page protector just large enough to lift them from the journaling. Don't be afraid to custom-cut your page protectors! I do this frequently and have never experienced my protectors tearing beyond the initial cut I made.

Along with my pocket page for stories, I added a collage page full of pictures with my closest friends throughout high school and college. When I look through albums of my mother, I love seeing pictures of her with her friends, laughing and having fun. It reminds me that she was young once and experienced the same kinds of things I did.

Additional School Story ideas: Were you in a school play you are proud of and want to share?
Do you have stories about being involved in sports or other extracurricular activities?
Maybe you are proud of the work you did on the yearbook or school newspaper.
Did you win any awards throughout your school years?
Perhaps you had problems with friends that you want to share with your children and describe how you resolved them. Make your stories encouraging, but genuine, so that your children can draw from your example.
Do you have regrets about not having been involved in different school activities? I will convey my thoughts on this to my children through this page in an effort to inspire them to reach higher for the activities they would like to experience.

College stories: Perhaps you would like to utilize this page as a means of encouragement for your children as it relates to college, and to endure, even during the most challenging times of this part of their lives.

Do you have special friends you would like to share with your children?
Create a page about you and your close friends and add pictures of all of you together. Consider having your friends write a brief note about you to add to this page. This will allow you to share your relationships with your children so that they can see how essential close

relationships with others are. If nothing else, it's always fun to read what others have to say about our parents!

If you do not live near some of your close friends, have them send you their notes. Consider providing them with the actual paper on which you want them to journal, and have them return it to you by mail. Through this process, you might even inspire them to begin a special album of their own!

What I am Proud of

Again, I used a pocket page so that I could add more journaling over time. I am sure I will encounter more things in life that I am proud of, and I want to be able to include them as they surface.

This was another page in which a photograph I found in my stock fit perfectly. I am very proud that I fulfilled one of my dreams of having a family, and all of my family members at this time are shown in the picture. I also chose to share with them how I worked two jobs right after high school graduation and how proud I was of purchasing my first car. I told my children that getting through college, even when I had thoughts of quitting, was a great accomplishment of mine. I shared with them how proud I am of my belief in God and of my values and morals that have guided my decisions through life.

What I'm
PROUD
of

Love Notes

I created this page as a means to collect and store all of the encouraging notes I intend to give my kids throughout their lives. I envision notes wishing them luck on days when they are in school, for example, and have an important test to take. Perhaps they will need encouragement before a big baseball game or gymnastics competition, or when they are involved in a spelling bee. These notes may not mean as much to my children when they are young, but how reassuring it will be for them to find them later on, and know that I supported them in all of their endeavors! I love to come across cards that my grandmothers had once written to me to encourage me in what I was doing. I know my children will enjoy the same. My boys already write on sticky notes and post them around my office and bedroom with scribbles that, to them, really are words! I love that they do this, and know that they will cherish finding all of the notes I wrote and saved for them while they were growing up.

Our Love, Mom & Dad

Don't forget to share with your children the relationship between you and their father. Believe it or not, some day they will want to know how you met, why you fell in love, and how you knew each other was the "right one." I think more than anything else, if my mother was still here and she and my father were still married, I would ask how they stayed together for so many years - what their "secret" was that held them together all this time. Although we can easily find marital advice in books and magazines, knowing what held my own parents together is what would really interest me. Just knowing these things about our own relatives makes it so much more meaningful, and seeing it with our own eyes can serve as an encouragement to apply the same ideals to our own lives.

This, however, may be a sensitive subject for some. Perhaps you do not have your children's father in your life. How do you explain this to them? Simply share your story to the extent at which you are comfortable, and tell your children what you want them to know about your past relationship with their father. Remember, they will not be reading this until they are older and likely have a better understanding of the difficult trials that can often encompass a relationship. There may be sections of this album you will show them as they are growing up, and others you may want to leave for them when they are older. Perhaps you had a special relationship with their father and you wish to emphasize that. If you have remarried, create a page about your new husband as well. I have two stepchildren of my own and, since

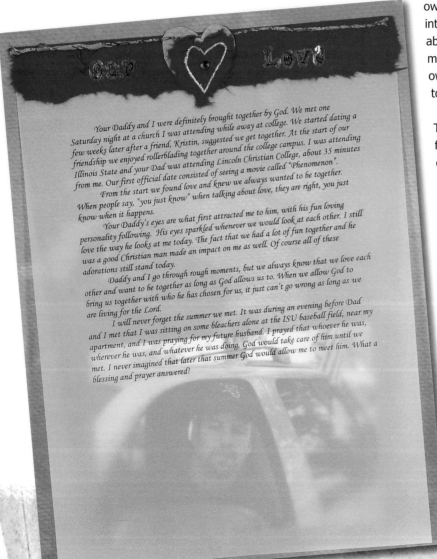

Your Daddy and I were definitely brought together by God. We met one Saturday night at a church I was attending while away at college. We started dating a few weeks later after a friend, Kristin, suggested we get together. At the start of our friendship we enjoyed rollerblading together around the college campus. I was attending Illinois State and your Dad was attending Lincoln Christian College, about 35 minutes from me. Our first official date consisted of seeing a movie called "Phenomenon".

From the start we found love and knew we always wanted to be together. When people say, "you just know" when talking about love, they are right, you just know when it happens.

Your Daddy's eyes are what first attracted me to him, with his fun loving personality following. His eyes sparkled whenever we would look at each other. I still love the way he looks at me today. The fact that we had a lot of fun together and he was a good Christian man made an impact on me as well. Of course all of these adorations still stand today.

Daddy and I go through rough moments, but we always know that we love each other and want to be together as long as God allows us to. When we allow God to bring us together with who he has chosen for us, it just can't go wrong as long as we are living for the Lord.

I will never forget the summer we met. It was during an evening before Dad and I met that I was sitting on some bleachers alone at the ISU baseball field, near my apartment, and I was praying for my future husband. I prayed that whoever he was, wherever he was, and whatever he was doing, God would take care of him until we met. I never imagined that later that summer God would allow me to meet him. What a blessing and prayer answered!

You may be a stepmother of children whom you see every day and with whom you share a special relationship. Don't forget to include them in your album, as they will feel special that you thought of them as if they were your own. There are a variety of family dynamics today. Decide what is best for your family and the steps you should take to create meaningful albums that fit your unique relationships.

What I most adore about Ty:
* He has a good, generous heart.
* He talks respectfully to others.
* Strives to do his best at everything he does.
* He is a hard worker and is very helpful to family
* And friends when they need help with projects.
* I love his muscles!

we do not get the opportunity to see them very often, I will create an album for them about their father rather than myself. In this album, I will display pictures of them together and have my husband write special notes to them that will be very meaningful one day.

Printing Tip

You may notice that, on many pages, I use my computer to journal my thoughts, then print them out on vellum. When you print what you have written, go into "properties" and select "other transparencies" for the paper. This will signal your printer to print it in such a way that it will not smear as easily on the vellum. Avoid touching the ink too soon, as it takes longer to dry on this type of paper.

Motherhood

Again, I chose to print my journaling on vellum for this page. I also used charms that represented what I wanted to say. The wheelbarrow represents how mothers carry many "loads" in life! The watering can represents how, as mothers, we pour on whatever emotion we are feeling, much of which is love! I chose to use this page as a means of communication to my children about what motherhood has meant to me. Although I want them to know how miraculous and wonderful my journey as a mother has been, I avoid sugar-coating it, as I want them to have a realistic picture of what mothering entails on a daily basis, both the good and the bad!

In addition to paragraphs, I wrote about my "picture" of motherhood and thought of several words to describe my mothering experiences. Though these will vary among all of us, think of your own descriptive words to illustrate how motherhood influences you.

To provoke my own thoughts, I took a few minutes to think of my days as a mother and contemplated my experiences with my children, the dynamics of my household, and my day-to-day duties. Just thinking of my life with toddlers brought everything I really wanted to say to the surface, and I simply wrote my thoughts on the page as they came to me. I have no doubt I will be adding more as I continue my journey through motherhood!

If you have grown children who are already out of the house and have families of their own, you may take a different approach to this page. For example, you may choose to create a page detailing what motherhood has been like for you, and use this page as an opportunity to bestow lots of motherly advice!

Motherhood

As a mother I carry many loads in life. Whether I work or stay home I take care of so many things. I take care of my home, nurture my children, take care of my husband in many ways, run the household tasks, and so much more. When you, my children, become a parent, you will know what all I am talking about. I love what I do, although it may not always seem that way. I could never hand this job over to anyone else. It's what is in me. I may get tired of picking up all the toys, but I would rather do it than to not have toys to pick up. Sometimes for an instant I forget that motherhood is a blessing, then I catch just a moment to myself and remember what God has given me to take care of and know that I have been truly blessed more than I could have ever imagined. One of my biggest joys of motherhood is watching you sleep. I love to do this because it gives me a chance to reflect on you and savor your moments in my mind. I am looking forward to being your mother for the rest of my life!

Besides carrying all of the loads, I as your mother, get to pour on the love or any emotion I am feeling. I need to take care of myself and find ways to fill myself up with positives so I can pour on the positives to everyone around me. I have to say I am not always full of positives, but I recognize when I am pouring out negatives. This makes our family atmosphere unpleasant. To me motherhood involves encouraging my family and pouring out encouragement all the time. I know that having this attitude will help our family to be close and loving. This is what I strive for.

Words to Describe My Motherhood
Here are words to describe things I do and how I sometimes feel as your mother.
(I am 27 at this time writing this and am sure some words will be added through the years!)

Challenging Encouraging Busy Productive Loving Caring
Frustrating Decisions Safety Tears Smiles Laughs Tickles
Discipline Kisses Hugs Playtime Reading Helping Work Tiring
Self Control Diapers Cooking Budgeting Paying Bills Shopping
Fun Chauffeur Humbling Satisfying Patience Listening Talking
Cheering Hard Angry Prayerful Worrisome Joyful

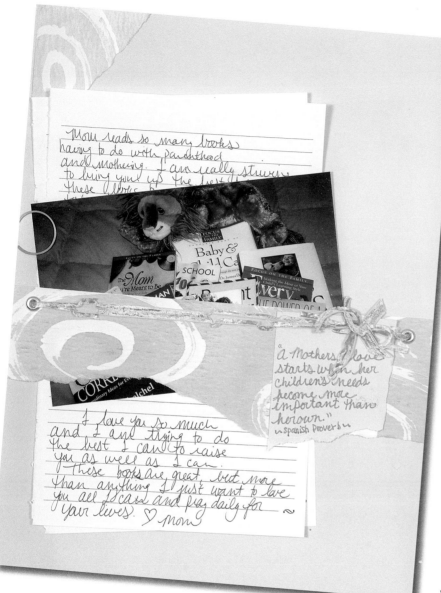

experiencing at the time. Just leave enough space to allow for room to add to them later. Maybe you would like to add a page about what you hope to accomplish as a mother, or one focusing on what kind of mother you strive to be. There are endless ways to approach this, all of which can be uniquely customized to fit your own thoughts.

Your children may need advice when they become a parent and want to know how you handled certain situations when they were young. Use this album to share your experiences with them! I would love to be able to call my mother and listen to how she handled my tantrums, for example, and have the opportunity to apply her advice to my own mothering endeavors. On the pocket page, I added a picture showing the many books I have read pertaining to motherhood and explained how I want to be the best mom I can be to them.

This is just one of many layouts I created without an idea in mind as to what picture I would implement into it. As it turned out, of course, the stock of photographs I had compiled before starting my album proved to hold the perfect image for this page! In fact, this is how the majority of my page content was inevitably fulfilled throughout my album. I am confident that they will fall into place for you in this manner as well.

Again, I added a pocket page to this layout since I know I will have varying thoughts at different stages of motherhood. This will allow me a very simple way to add those thoughts through journaling. You will likely find that there are other ways to create pages pertaining to what mothering stage you are going through. If you come up with an idea, you would simply add pages similar to the one you created first, and alter the title slightly as it relates to the unique stage you are

My American Dream

I used this page to talk about the things in life that make it so enjoyable for me. Use this page as an opportunity to share with your children your American Dream and what makes life pleasurable for you. For me, it is driving to the local ice cream stand with my family on a hot summer night, getting the mail, taking occasional afternoon naps, cooking meals for my family, and watching them enjoy it. For this page, I wrote my list in my own handwriting and included one extra piece of journal paper so that I could continue to add more until I give the album to my children. This page is so simple that an original could easily be created for each child's album.

Get Started

What do you really enjoy in life? Make a list of your current passions.

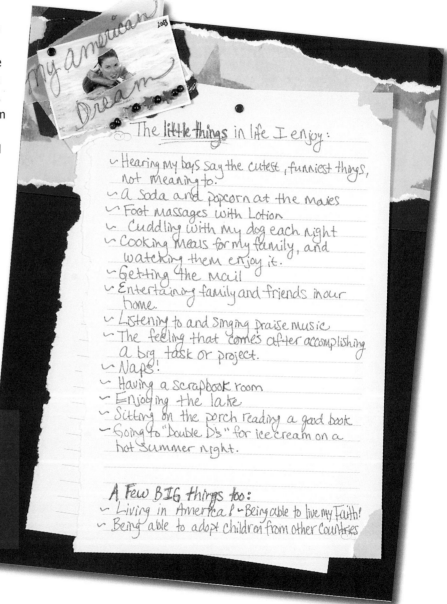

The little things in life I enjoy:

- Hearing my boys say the cutest, funniest things, not meaning to.
- A soda and popcorn at the movies
- Foot massages with lotion
- Cuddling with my dog each night
- Cooking meals for my family, and watching them enjoy it.
- Getting the mail
- Entertaining family and friends in our home.
- Listening to and singing praise music
- The feeling that comes after accomplishing a big task or project.
- Naps!
- Having a scrapbook room
- Enjoying the lake
- Sitting on the porch reading a good book
- Going to "Double D's" for ice cream on a hot summer night.

A Few BIG things too:
- Living in America! ~ Being able to live my Faith!
- Being able to adopt children from other countries

Work

Since the age of 16, I have already worn a variety of hats in terms of work, and I know that I will try a few more different kinds of jobs before I reach retirement age. I felt that it was important for my children to know what kinds of jobs I have worked, what I liked about them, and what I disliked about them. If you have not yet experienced working outside of the home during your parenting tenure, though you know you would like to some day, consider creating a page describing what you think you might enjoy doing as a career in the future. Perhaps you completed training in a specific field prior to having children, but have not yet chosen to execute your knowledge in the form of a fulltime career until your children are older. I have my teaching certificate, but have not yet been employed as a schoolteacher. I will use this page as an opportunity to share this information with my children and detail my long-term goals in this area. I also want my children to know that hard work is essential in life, and that someday, they

will discover something they enjoy, though they may experience many different trades until they find the perfect one. Whatever your work story may be, share it with your children. You may be surprised to find that they have gained valuable messages from your example, and one day, may even walk in your footsteps!

On this page, I utilized the back of a tag to list all the jobs I have had up to this point in my life. I also added a few recent pictures of me working at scrapbook events.

I wrote on the back of the matted pictures, in detail, what I was doing and why I enjoy doing it. For instance, in one of the pictures, I am hosting my first organized crop, which drew over 150 attendants. I wrote to my children about how I enjoy event planning, particularly in the scrapbook industry. Since I used a pocket on this page, I will be able to add more work-related pictures and journaling in the future.

Inspiring Verses

I chose to add this page because faith is an important part of my life. I want my children to know what Bible verses were special to me and how God has used them in my life. Below are some excerpts taken from my own journaling:

"Then Jesus declared, 'I am the bread of life. He who comes to me will never go hungry, and he who believes in me will never be thirsty.'" John 6:35
This verse is so true! I used to think this verse means that God will always take care of me, because He always has in every way, financially, emotionally, and otherwise. I now know, through getting to know my Lord more, that, not only will He always meet our needs, He is all I need! He is my bread and my water. I will never need anything else because I have Him.

"A generous man will himself be blessed, for he shares his food with the poor." Proverbs 22:9
I have a heart to give. This verse is important because it tells us it is right to give to others, and not just to the poor or less unfortunate. We must allow ourselves to open our hearts to this. It is important to resist giving because you are told to, but to focus on giving because it is in your heart.

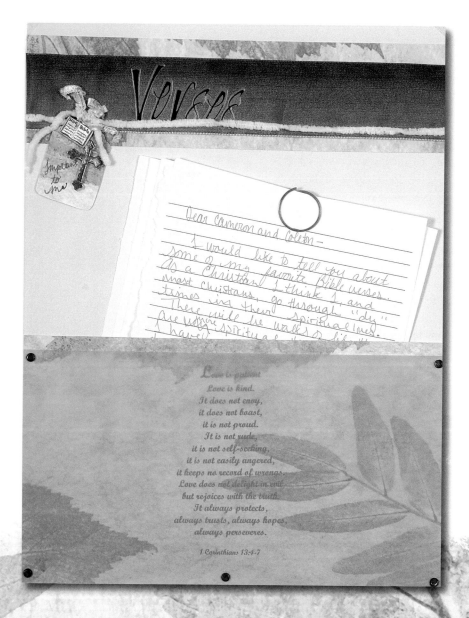

Love is patient.
Love is kind.
It does not envy,
it does not boast,
it is not proud.
It is not rude,
it is not self-seeking,
it is not easily angered,
it keeps no record of wrongs.
Love does not delight in evil
but rejoices with the truth.
It always protects,
always trusts, always hopes,
always perseveres.

1 Corinthians 13:4-7

My Prayers for You

This is another important page to me. I want my children to know that I pray for them. As they grow older, they will be able to see what I prayed for on their behalf, and which of those prayers were answered for them. I created another pocket page in this layout, this time using ribbon as embellishment. Creating a pocket like this is so simple! It simply entailed layering three pieces of wide ribbon and utilizing glue dots to adhere them to the back of the page. I stitched buttons into the middle of the pocket so that I could have two separate pockets. I also stitched the bottom of the ribbon to keep my journaling inside the pocket. A very easy and decorative pocket made out of ribbon! I will place the prayers in the pocket and, as they are answered, move it to the side of the pocket labeled, "Answered." What a great way for my children to see how God answers our prayers and works in our lives!

You may have different inspirational pages in mind to create for your children. By all means, go for it! Follow your heart and create what comes naturally!

This is another example of using a favorite picture from my photograph stock. I was unsure of where I would use this picture of Coleton, and after I created this page, I knew it would fit perfectly on it. Since one of my prayers for Coleton is that God would open all of the right doors for him, the picture of him climbing into our armoire was just right! I cherish this picture and how it suits my thoughts on this page so perfectly!

A Prayer for My Daughter

Although I do not yet have a daughter, I made a Prayer Page for her, too. I know I will have her with me some day, and it helps to journal my prayers for her now. I created this page knowing she will someday know how I prayed for her, even before I met her. Because the journal pages are fastened to the page with only brads, I can add more journal paper to the layout as I need it. If you did not notice through my journaling on this page, my husband and I are hoping to adopt our daughter from China in a few years. I know this page will mean a lot to her when she grows old enough to understand what had taken place before her arrival. I love the quote at the bottom of the vellum on this page, taken from Abraham Lincoln: "I remember my mother's prayers and they have always followed me. They have clung to me all my life."

Another page idea in this category would be to create a page sharing how God has moved in your life. If faith happens to be a significant part of your life, your children will benefit from knowing the unique ways God has worked in your life. If you have shared heartfelt journaling throughout your album, they may have already seen many of those examples, so this would be a wonderful page to create as a supplement to sharing these wonderful thoughts about your walk!

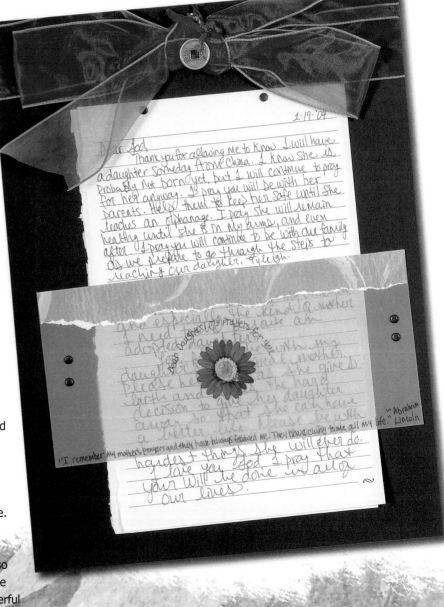

Purpose

I created this page because this subject was something close to my heart that I wanted to share with my children. For me, coming to the realization of the purpose of my life has been a bit of a struggle. I needed to share this with my children in the event they experience similar feelings, and so that they have a better understanding of who I am. Another way to be real with the people we love! If there are things close to your heart that you would like to share with your children, this album is the perfect opportunity to accomplish just that. It may not be about "purpose," but something entirely different. Only you know what is truly important to you, and only you can share that information.

As you may notice, this page consists solely of journaling. I have considered adding another page to this layout at a later time once we have completed our family. At that time, I will include a picture of me with each child to the extra page. This will be a layout that I will color copy for each additional child, rather than each receiving their own original.

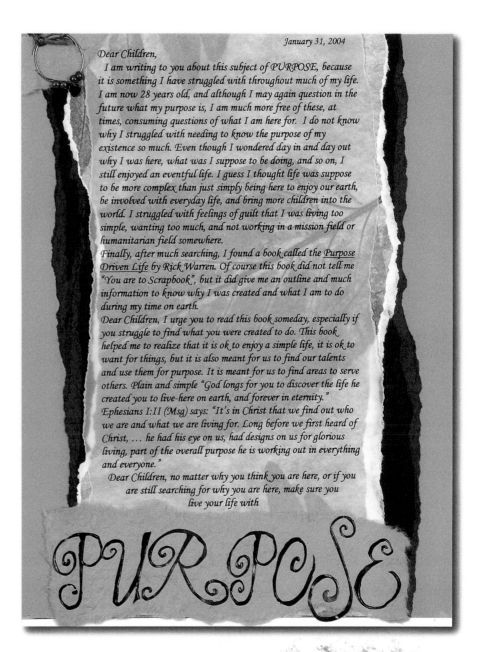

January 31, 2004

Dear Children,
  I am writing to you about this subject of PURPOSE, because it is something I have struggled with throughout much of my life. I am now 28 years old, and although I may again question in the future what my purpose is, I am much more free of these, at times, consuming questions of what I am here for. I do not know why I struggled with needing to know the purpose of my existence so much. Even though I wondered day in and day out why I was here, what was I suppose to be doing, and so on, I still enjoyed an eventful life. I guess I thought life was suppose to be more complex than just simply being here to enjoy our earth, be involved with everyday life, and bring more children into the world. I struggled with feelings of guilt that I was living too simple, wanting too much, and not working in a mission field or humanitarian field somewhere.

Finally, after much searching, I found a book called the Purpose Driven Life by Rick Warren. Of course this book did not tell me "You are to Scrapbook", but it did give me an outline and much information to know why I was created and what I am to do during my time on earth.

Dear Children, I urge you to read this book someday, especially if you struggle to find what you were created to do. This book helped me to realize that it is ok to enjoy a simple life, it is ok to want for things, but it is also meant for us to find our talents and use them for purpose. It is meant for us to find areas to serve others. Plain and simple "God longs for you to discover the life he created you to live-here on earth, and forever in eternity."

Ephesians 1:11 (Msg) says: "It's in Christ that we find out who we are and what we are living for. Long before we first heard of Christ, ... he had his eye on us, had designs on us for glorious living, part of the overall purpose he is working out in everything and everyone."

  Dear Children, no matter why you think you are here, or if you are still searching for why you are here, make sure you live your life with

PURPOSE

Where Did You Get That Personality?

Where did You get that Personality?

YES

There are some things that I hope you acquire from me. I hope you take from me my good stubbornness. I can be stubborn sometimes when I really believe in what I am talking about. It is hard to change my mind when this happens! I hope you have the strength and will to always believe in what you believe and not to give it up easily. If you are like me you will be hardworking, have an eagerness to learn, be kind and generous, and you will have the drive to never give up on your ambitions and dreams. Please have faith in God like I do and have a melting heart for people in need. I hope you too will be a person that strives to be of integrity, honesty, and make decisions to do what is right. I hope that my desire to have a healthy lifestyle rubs off on you.

If you are like me you will strive to be a leader.

I hope you acquire all the good traits I have and so many more! All these good things come from God and that is who we ultimately strive to be like. What I really want you to do is be your own person. Only be influenced in ways that make you a better person. I look forward to watching you grow up and seeing what a great young man you are going to be, although, you will always be my little boy.

NO

Just as there are traits I hope you acquire from me, there are some I wish you do not!

Please do not have my "bad" stubbornness! Sometimes I can be too stubborn. Like when I really need to compromise, but don't. You will know when this happens, you can choose to do the right thing.

Sometimes I have a one track mind, please have the ability to open your mind and see from all sides. Please be very outgoing. Although I am more outgoing than some people, I tend to be shy a lot too. I stay in my own world instead of venturing out when I should. Please venture out as much as you can, you will go far and see things you would not get to if you stayed in your own little corner of the world. I hope you think "out of the box". One thing I just cannot stand is that my mind just gets stuck in the box. I am frustrated when my thinking and creativity just cannot go farther than I would.

I hope you are just so creative, bright and artsy. I do not see myself as artistic, and oh how I wish I was! I hope you are a huge "book worm" at an early age. I did not read much as a child and teenager, although I sure like to read now. As a result I do not have the kind of vocabulary I wish I had. I feel confined to basic words and I would love to use big lovely words that really make people think! Having such a small vocabulary really makes me feel like I am stuck on a small island as opposed to having the whole world to explore.

Sometimes mom is too quickly angered. That is something I hope I do not pass down to you. I am working on that in me and I hope that by teaching you what is right, I can fix what I'm doing wrong in myself as well. You are such a gift, you help me so much, to be a better person, when it seems like I am suppose to be helping you!

Many of these things I am telling you not to acquire from me can be avoided in you. None of us are perfect and we do not need to try to be. But, when we are acting in a way we know we should not be acting, it can be avoided. I will help you and guide you to become the best person you can be, always improving through life. I believe growing in every way is a life long process and we develop every day of our lives. God has a plan for us and He prepares us and equips us with exactly what He wants us to have as long as we allow Him to and seek out His gifts for us.

One thing to remember, just know that you are a great person that has been given many talents and gifts. Sometimes we wish we can have talents that we see in other people, but we have our own talents. I do believe that we each have many talents that just show up through our life and we did not even know they existed. Just keep searching and doing the best you can at what interests you. God will reward you for that.

It was important for me to highlight my children's personality traits and where they came from. I am thankful for some of the traits my kids have acquired from me, though there are some I wish they hadn't!

I have been told many times that I stand in a similar fashion that my mother frequently did. I sometimes stand with one foot propped up on my other knee, when I am in the kitchen cooking or leaning against a wall. Since my mother is not here, I feel comforted when people tell me about the traits she and I share. It makes me feel good that, in some ways, I am like her. How fun it will be for your children to discover the ways they are similar to you through this page in their album! As my children grow, I may find pictures that compliment this page and add them on a page opposite this one.

This may be a more challenging page to create for the children my husband and I plan to adopt in the future. In this case, I would most likely create a page in many of the same ways, sharing what I would like for them to acquire from me in terms of personality. While I may not be able to share heredity-based traits with them, I'm sure I will influence them in many ways simply by virtue of our day-to-day interactions.

Favorite Pictures of You

Throughout your child's life, you may find pictures of them that you love and treasure. This is important, as our children will want to know which photographs we cherished most. Having some of these photographs already, I created a mini photo album on which to adhere these photos. You may also want to add journaling to the mini album and describe why you love those particular pictures so much. When finished, I placed the mini album in a pocket that will hold it forever. This will allow me to add more of my favorite pictures later without having to use a significant amount of space in my album. When my children want to look at the pictures, all they have to do is pull the mini album out of the pocket on this page, which, of course, is in a page protector.

On this page, I created a pocket out of mulberry paper. To hold the mini album inside, I threaded wire through the bottom of the paper just as I would with thread. I strung beads on the wire as I went along.

I chose to create my own mini album rather than buying one because I wanted it to match the color of paper I was using. Additionally, with the task of making one for each child, it proved to be more cost effective to make my own. The only supplies needed to make the album were two pieces of cardstock and some fiber. I used a single hole punch to position the holes precisely where I need them. I also used a Coluzzle® cutting system to make a hole on the front of the album so that my picture could be seen.

Things I Want to Tell You

With this page, I decided to take pictures that would allow me to share with my children things I think they should hear from me. In this layout, I included messages I wanted to impart to them throughout their lives. For example, using photographs of Coleton trying to climb up and stand next to the bathtub, I chose to relay the message, "Never stop trying." I want my kids to know that, no matter how difficult situations are in their lives, they should never give up. I think of these as "pictures with a purpose," and found that it's interesting how we can use photographs to teach our kids important messages. I also added journaling to demonstrate to them some of the important lessons they will need throughout their lives – little messages of encouragement from my heart.

You may be wondering what Coleton is doing in the picture of him bending down to the ground as if he is kissing it. One evening when Ty, my husband, was washing the car, Coleton decided he was thirsty. Instead of asking mom for something to drink, he squatted down to the driveway to drink the water out of the little holes in the cement! As he was only 15 months at the time, I was in shock at what I was seeing! A scrapbooker at heart, I ran to capture a picture first, and afterwards, told him to stop drinking the water from the driveway (fortunately, the soap from the car had not yet reached his little personal reservoir)! I used these pictures to encourage him to have fun in life and to always think "outside the box!" Little boy brains never cease to amaze me! I also added some thoughts in a hidden journal box for Coleton, which, in order to read it, will have to be untied by him.

Since my kids are still so young, I know I will accumulate more pictures in the future, which will serve as inspirations from which to offer them messages of encouragement and support. As they accrue, I will create more pages to accommodate them. If you have older children and already have many of those pictures, it may be easier to do what I did on the second page. Simply write the messages on the back using journal paper, and place them in a pocket. I am sure you will visualize creative ways to share your special messages!

In the past, I have laminated the pictures with journaling on the back using the Zyron®. I chose to do this because I suspected little fingers would someday be handling these pictures, and I knew they would become covered with fingerprints without protection. This is simply an idea you can choose to implement in an effort to protect various elements of your album. When my children want to see the pictures and read what I have to share on the back, they can pull them out of the page protector. You may also choose to cut a slit in the page protector to allow for easier access.

Things I Want to Tell You

On another page of this layout, I chose to put the pictures in a pocket. I found photographs I adored of my boys and knew that I could reveal little messages of encouragement for them through these pictures. I mounted them on cardstock and adhered journaling paper on the back. I wrote things I wanted to tell them and messages that the pictures inspired me to share, an example of which you can see on this page.

I Am Proud of You

It is so important for our children to know we are proud of them and, even more importantly, why. Through the years, I want to make sure I document the many ways my children make me proud of them. I may see them helping people who are in need some day, and it will invoke strong feelings of pride for them. There will be many reasons to document, and I want my children to know, in detail, what they are.

Below is my first journal entry for Cameron:

Cameron, today Mom taught you how to write our last name. You had it down in no time! You are such an eager learner! I am so proud of you for working hard in pre-school to learn your name and letters.

If your children are older, or are already adults with families of their own, you can still go back and think of all the things that have made you proud of them. Recall those special moments of their childhood, and make a point to share with them what made you so proud. Include events from their past that have touched you through the years. It is never too late to share these thoughts with them!

I Love Being With You

I used these pages to share with my kids the many things I enjoy doing with them, and added pictures of us together. As we continue to share life together, I anticipate many more photographs to capture our special memories, and will add them as I move forward with the albums. How important it is that our children know we enjoyed spending time with them, no matter how irrelevant our activities together seemed! Just recently, Cameron, my 5 year old, learned how to open the application, Word, on our computer. He watches me type frequently and found that he loves to type as well! Since he is in preschool and just now starting to show an interest in letters, he would type a letter on the computer and ask me to write it on a piece of paper. I had no idea why he wanted me to do this for him, but he was persuasive, so I complied! He would type the letters and numbers, and I would, in turn, write them for him on paper. This outwardly mundane activity we did together was actually quite fun, and I know we both enjoyed each other. I'm sure that this is a memory he will

making Dad's B.D. cake.

carry for some time until his small world begins to grow, at which time, he'll need my album to remind him of this, as well as the other meaningful activities we enjoyed together.

Almost every day, I hear someone express how fast time goes by and to "enjoy every minute you have." While I know I can't stop time, each year seems to go by faster and faster. I am trying to enjoy every minute I spend with my family, and I know that this album for them will live on much longer than I will. My children will be able to look back and see just how meaningful our lives together were, and know how much they were loved. Most of all, I will know that what I stood for in life will be passed on through my legacy. I truly believe, with all of my heart, that my album will pass through the hands for which they were intended, and that the generations yet to come will be encouraged by what I have left for them.

On the first page with Coleton, I added pictures of the two of us enjoying activities together. I reduced the picture sizes on my computer so that I could fit more pictures on one page. As time goes on, I can add more pages with new pictures we accumulate. The photo mat opens up to reveal my journaling and more photographs of activities we share

together. I even like to use the little index pictures I receive with my developed prints to accomplish this because they are so small. I loved finally finding a use for those little pictures, which are also handy for tags!

I Love Being With You

On the next layout, I used another pocket to hold my journaling. I used a mini book created from folded cardstock to hold more pictures of Cameron and I enjoying each other. Again, I resized the pictures and used journal paper to describe the activities we were doing together and index prints to allow for more pictures. Our family loves to go to the root beer stand together in the warmer seasons, where we enjoy ordering food to eat in our car. It is truly one of our favorite activities to do together, and I wanted to share this with my children to convey to them how much I enjoy this time together. This mini book, and the small photos that accompany it, allow me to share this with them without consuming a significant amount of space.

Mom's Thoughts at Age...

I created this pocket page to include my thoughts at certain ages, and will continue to add to it every 5 years or so. This will allow me to talk about anything I want to say during various phases of my life. This page will be beneficial to your children because they might want to look back at you at a certain age and know what was going on in your life, and the decisions you have faced throughout the years. They may find themselves apprehensive to enter into their 40's or 50's and will be able to discover your thoughts at that age and possibly learn that they are facing some of the same challenges. As I approach the age of 30, I find myself trying to decide on the best place to send my children to school, and reflect on the time during which they won't be here with me all day. Will I go to work outside of the home? Will I engage in volunteer-based activities? I also find myself speculating on how to space out the birth or adoption of my future children and what timing would be best for our family. Another issue that has become a source of apprehension for me is that I am approaching the age of my mother at the time she was diagnosed with breast cancer. It would be comforting for my daughters to know how I coped with this so that if they find themselves experiencing the same fear, they will be armed with the knowledge of what calmed me during that time.

As you can see, I included a picture of myself alone. Over time, as I age, I will add other pictures of myself by placing them in the pocket. For the journaling, I used paper from a journal, included my age at the top, and simply added my writing. To add more journaling after my kids receive the albums, I will give it to them to add to the pocket pages as I have done in the past.

45

My Two Cents

This page is reserved for what we mothers do best: give advice! What a great opportunity to share it with them at a time they will most need it! This section will provide a straightforward way for our children to know how we handled a variety of situations, right at their fingertips!

I used another pocket for adding journaling cards when I think of advice to share with them. Topics you may wish to include are friends, school, dating, finances, and marriage. I cut cardstock the size of index cards and wrote my journaling on them. Store-bought index cards should be safe to use as an alternative as long as your pictures will not come in direct contact with them. You may choose to use a real envelope for this page, or envelope templates that are available in stores.

I continued my layout with another page entitled, "Lessons I Have Learned." I know I will want to share the lessons I've learned during my life with my children and, by using a pocket and journaling paper, I can add more as time goes on. I chose to create a very simple page for this because, to me, my thoughts are the most important aspect of this section.

Album Contents

Album Contents

Introduction
Leaving My Legacy
Mom's Favorite Things
I Hope to Make a Difference
Mom's Childhood
Mom's School Stories
Dreams and Goals
Mom's Challenges Through Life
What I'm Proud Of
Our Love; Mom & Dad
Motherhood
My American Dream
Mom's Thoughts at Age...
Verses Important to Me
My Prayers for You
Where Did You Get That Personality
What's Your Purpose?
Favorite Pictures of You
Things I Want to Tell You
What Makes Me Proud of You
I Would Like to Share With You...
I Love Being With You!
My 2 Cents
Lessons I've Learned
Love Notes
End Note

This page is not a requirement, but is a start to a theme album. Essentially, it is a list of the pages, in sequence, contained in your album. While this particular layout will be placed at the beginning of your album, I have included my thoughts on this page toward the end of this book because it is a page you may not be able to complete until your album in finished. It may be helpful to keep a rough list of page titles and layouts on a separate piece of paper until your project is complete, at which time you can construct this page in its entirety and place it at the beginning of your album.

End Note

This last page was created to let my children know how I felt while creating this album for them. I feel blessed that I could write out my thoughts and feelings to them, and I find peace in knowing that, one day when I'm not here to share them, they will know my own thoughts and feelings through this album.

In addition to putting this album together for my children, creating it has also helped me. I never really understood what people meant by trying to "find themselves." I now understand the meaning behind those words. By creating these albums about myself, I have gotten to know myself on a deeper level, and am beginning to understand just who this person inside of me really is. I believe that this is important, as my goal in creating this album is to leave a legacy for my children. Through this process, I now have a clear perception of what I want that legacy to be.

It has truly been a remarkable process for me. I wish the same for you. Whatever your journey may entail through creating your own pages, it will be a rewarding one.

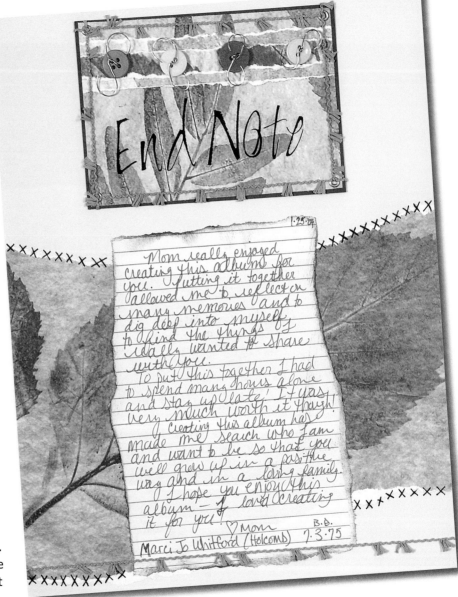

Mom really enjoyed creating this album for you. Putting it together allowed me to reflect on many memories and to dig deep into myself to find the things I really wanted to share with you.

To put this together I had to spend many hours alone and stay up late! It was very much worth it though!

Creating this album has made me search who I am and want to be so that you will grow up in a positive way and in a loving family. I hope you enjoy this album — I loved creating it for you!

♡ Mom

Marci Jo Whitford (Holcomb) 7.3.75   B.D.

Section Three

It's time to start your own!

Now that you have finished reading this book, it's time to get started with creating your special legacy albums for your children. Although it may seem overwhelming, take one step at a time and go back through each page section, one at a time. Before you know it, you will be at the end and your album will be complete for the time being. Keep in mind, however, that even after you finish all of your pages, maintenance is essential. Simply remember to go back when you find things to share with your children, and add your journaling and any new pictures as time goes by. If you ever find yourself in need of help or encouragement with your album, you can e-mail me anytime at marci@remindersoffaith.com.

Album Checklist

_____Buy or create a journal.

_____Start journaling questions to ask yourself.

_____Reflect on all the things you would want your children to know about you if you were not here to tell them. Write it all down in your journal.

_____Choose what size albums you would like to pass on to your children.

_____Make a list of all the pages you want in this album. It is to be expected that you will think of more while working on the album.

_____Decide on your favorite colors and how you want the style of your album to flow together.

_____Shop for paper and embellishments.

_____Go through all of your pictures not yet scrapped. If you do not have any because you are caught up on your other albums, make a list of pictures to take for this album.

_____Take additional pictures you want in this album (see other handout for ideas).

_____Make copies of pictures you will need duplicates of.

_____Choose motivational music that will help you get into the right mood for this album. This album can provoke feelings of strong emotions, and you really have to look deep within yourself to bring to the surface all the things you want to tell your children. You should find a way that works for you and allows you to accomplish this.

_____Start creating one page at a time with the help from the list of pages you made. Simply keep working until you're finished! Refer to this book as many times as you find necessary to help you with your pages. You will be so proud of yourself and happy with the results! Avoid making this project so elaborate that you become overwhelmed and postpone it. Keep it simple enough so you'll be sure to finish it. You can always go back later and add things that might look nice. Balance out the pages; some may be very simple, but charming, and others may require more detailed work.

You are done for now! Keep up with it through the years!

Picture Ideas

After you have gone through all of your photos and picked out your favorites, you may find that there are still pictures that need to be taken. Below are some ideas of photographs you may need:

- Obtain a current picture of you with each of your children; all together and individually.

- Include a picture of you by yourself; make sure that it is current so that your children know what you looked like when you started this album.

- Take pictures of your children alone; include close-ups and those in which they are engaged in activities you love to seem them doing.

- Take pictures of your children that would represent the things you wish to share with them. Example: A picture of a child taking his first steps could be used to encourage him to persevere or work hard in life.

- Choose a few pictures of yourself during childhood and those of family members, friends, or pets you would like to include in the album on your childhood page.

- Be sure to include pictures taken of you while working on this album.

You will also find that it may be easier to take some of these pictures as you need them. For example, you might be working on a page about your child and decide to include a photograph of his favorite toy, at which time you can simply take this picture of him with it to include in the page.

Make a list of the pictures you think you will need for your album.

Creating a Father's Legacy Album

Now that you have completed your album for your children, you may wish to think about creating a special album about your children's father. You can create it the same way you created your own, or you can choose to create one for the kids to share.

Approach it in the same manner in which you created your own legacy album. All of the same shopping will need to be accomplished, but ask your children's father what colors he would like to represent him. If you already know many details about him, you can choose embellishments to match the album colors and representation of him. For example, I chose some baseball and fishing embellishments that would coordinate with my husband's color scheme and represent the things he enjoys doing.

In most cases, Dad may not want to actually sit down and create the album himself, but his input into the project is important so that his album conveys little touches of his personality and unique viewpoint of his children. This will also make him feel included in the process when his children are presented with this album.

Rather than asking him to sit down and journal to his kids, ask him specific questions and write down his thoughts for him. Consider giving him journal pages complete with questions, and ask him to write to the kids about those particular subjects so that his album, too, contains samples of his own handwriting. This will show your children that their dad involved himself in this project, and that he had a hand in creating it for them. Show Dad the finished pages as they are completed. Ask him for his input and how he feels about them. This way, he feels like an active participant in the album, which will make it more special to him.

Enjoy participating in this album together! If this is something that is difficult to do together for personal reasons, perhaps you can give him some journaling paper to fill out and return to you so that you can arrange them into the album for your children.

This project may be challenging in some situations, such as those involving divorce. Ask yourself what your children would want to know about their dad if he was not here to share his thoughts with them. They may be young at the time, but will ask questions about their father as they grow older. This is natural process with children that is virtually inevitable, as we all eventually experience a natural curiosity about our parents!

If your child's father has passed away, and you are unsure about how he would have answered many of the questions, you can still create an album about him. Just reflect on what you do know, and make a list of the pages you could create about him. Perhaps you could enlist the help of his family and friends to get more information about him to use in the album.

Have fun! You might just learn some things about your children's father that you never knew!

Daddy's Unconditional Love

Daddy's
Unconditional
Love

For this page, I wanted to highlight how much my husband and boys love being together, as well as some activities they enjoy together. I shared with my husband, Ty, what I wanted to express to the boys through this page. He then thought of his own journaling telling our boys how much he enjoys being with them, and how much he loves them, unconditionally.

About the Author

Passing on Your Legacy of Love is written by Marci Whitford, mother to Cameron and Coleton, and wife to Ty. Marci lives in Pekin, Illinois and is an active participant in various conventions and workshops related to the Scrapbooking industry. She plans events in her region such as the "Pink Ribbon Crop," organized to benefit breast cancer foundations and bus tours to scrapbook stores among the Midwest states. Marci enjoys meeting scrapbookers and is excited that so many women share the love of this valuable hobby with her. Her passion is to encourage women to pass on special personalized albums to their children, detailing for them the many aspects of their lives. You can find Marci's workshops on which this book is based at various events and stores around the United States, or visit www.remindersoffaith.com, an organization for which Marci serves as a design team member, for more information. If you are interested in scheduling any of Marci's classes or workshops for your store or organization, you may contact her at marci@remindersoffaith.com.

Product Credits

Unless otherwise noted, all patterned papers used in the page layouts throughout this book are from Reminders of Faith's Leaves, Royal, and Colors collections. All Tag Embellishments are also from Reminders of Faith, with specific titles noted in the credits below. All fibers used are from Ties That Bind, all cardstock shown is from Chantilly Lace, and all lined journaling paper is from Canson.

Page 12
Font: LD Antique Letter. Stickers: Creative Imaginations. Ribbon: Offray. Beads: Bead Treasures.

Page 13
Font: CK Script. Mini Frame: Bead Treasures.

Page 18
Tag line: Reminder's of Faith, "Love". Font: 2Peas, "Beautiful" Beads: Freckle Press. Ribbon: Offray.

Page 19
Specialty Paper: Pressed Petals Sticker.

Page 20 & 21
Tag line :Reminders of Faith, "Hope". Ribbon: Offray Font: CK Journaling, "LD Curly", 2Peas, "Moonbeams".

Page 22 & 23
Fiber: Fibers by the Yard, Scrapbooks-n-Stickers. Letter Stickers: Provocraft. Wedge black Alphabities.

Page 24
Letters: Stampin' Up. Ribbon: Offray. Beads: Jewel Craft. Designer Beads: Memory Wire.

Page 25:
Tag Line: Reminders of Faith, "Love". Letter Stickers: Creative Imaginations Mulberry Paper: Legacy Paper. Mini-envelope: Hero Arts.
Wire word: Card Creations. Letter Stickers: Provocraft. Background Stamp: Paper Inspirations.

Page 26 & 27
Font: Mono Script. Letter Stickers: Provocraft. Background Stamp: Paper Inspirations.

Page 28
Charms: Charming Pages. Title: Deluxe Cut.

Page 30
Stars: Bead Treasures.

Page 31
Tag Line: Reminders of Faith, "Family". Letter Stickers: Creative Imaginations.

Page 32
Tag Line: Reminders of Faith, "Hope". Letter Stickers: Creative Imaginations. Charm: Charming Accents.

Page 33
Letter Stickers: Provocraft. Crosses: Jewel Craft.

Page 34
Ribbon: Finishing Touches. Flower Sticker: Pressed Petals. (Accent-Asian coin)

Page 35
Font: Monotype Corsiva. Letter Stickers: Creative Imaginations. Wire: Memory Beads.

Page 36
Letter Stickers: Creative Imaginations. Beads: Create-a-Craft Beads, "Blue Santa Beads".

Page 37
Letters: Laser Letters.

Page 38-40:
Letter Stickers: Creative Imaginations. Ribbon: Offray.

Page 42-44
Tag Line: Reminders of Faith, "Joy". Paper: Reminders of Faith, "Illusions".

Page 45
Letter Stickers: Creative Imaginations.

Page 46
Letter Stickers: Sticopotomus. Ribbon: Offray. Envelope: Paper Adventures.

Page 47
Font: Andy. Beads: Bead Treasures.

Page 48
Tag Line: Reminders of Faith, "Hope". Letter Stickers: Creative Imaginations.

Company Contacts

Reminders Of Faith *(publisher, scrapbook products)*
contact: Kathy Brundage
www.remindersoffaith.com
Kathyb@remindersoffaith.com
412-720-2699

Chantilly Lace *(cardstock)*
contact: Marc Chabot
http://www.chantillylacecrafts.com
866-803-0471

First Impressions Printing
contact: Todd Williams
Pittsburgh, PA
412-488-3800

Reeves Digital Development *(website)*
contact: Cindy Reeves
www.reevesdigital.com
cindy@reevesdigital.com

Palermo Imaging *(photography)*
contact: Paul Palermo
www.palermoimaging.com
724-940-0039

Ties That Bind *(fiber company)*
contact: Gary and Sharon Stone
www.tiesthatbindfiber.com
505-762-0295

Reminders of Faith™

Mail order form to: 518 Overhead Drive
Moon Township, Pa 15108
Or fax your order form to: Fax: 412-264-7857
Email questions to: orders@remindersoffaith.com
www.remindersoffaith.com

Shipping Information:

Name	
Address	
City, State Zip	
Email	
Phone	

QUANTITY	DESCRIPTION	UNIT PRICE	TOTAL
	Passing On Your Legacy of Love	$14.95	

	SUBTOTAL	
Please add 7% sales tax for PA orders	**TAX**	
Shipping is $4.00 per order	**SHIPPING**	
	BALANCE DUE	

Thank you for purchasing "Passing On Your Legacy of Love". We hope this book inspires you to tell your own story of God's Faithfulness in your life. We would love to hear from you. Please email your comments to: marci@remindersoffaith.com

Credit card number:
Expiration date:
Circle one: Visa   MasterCard   Discover
Print Name on card:

_____
Signature

Please make checks payable to: Reminders Of Faith